ALZHEIMER'S GIFTS

Very best!

Rick Naymark

ALZHEIMER'S GIFTS

by

RICK NAYMARK

Alzheimer's Gifts
© 2016 by Rick Naymark

ISBN: 978-0-578-18512-5

Library of Congress Control Number: 2016915873

About the author
Rick Naymark lives in Minnesota, where he is a writer and marketing consultant. He is married and has three children.

Special thanks
The author thanks those who gave editing and content advice, and encouragement, including Joan Naymark, Roger Gefvert, Earl Hipp, Gary Legwold, Dave Kamminga and John Ziegenhagen. My mother's last years were spent at a competent and loving care facility called Jones Harrison Residence, in Minneapolis, and I will forever be thankful to them.

Sources of quotations
Familiar Quotations, John Bartlett, 11th Ed., Christopher Morley, editor, Little, Brown and Company, 1938.
The Harper Book of Quotations, 3rd Ed., Robert I. Fitzhenry, editor, Quil/HarperResources, 1993.
Quotes Every Man Should Know, Nick Mamatus, editor, Quirk Productions, Inc., 2013.

Out of respect
Names of Alzheimer care facility residents have been changed for the sake of their privacy; the incidents narrated are real.

Published by:

 **Gentili** Press

Contents

To my wife Joan and my sister Jean,
who were steadfast companions on this
journey.

FOREWORD

THE purpose of this book is to share the unexpected gifts I experienced caring for a loved one with Alzheimer's. These gifts helped me turn a difficult situation into a positive experience.

The job of caring for a loved one is not for the weak at heart. Alzheimer's wards are, to various degrees, almost haunting. Residents shuffle like ghosts of themselves. The healthier ones wander the halls looking for their rooms, wanting to go home without the slightest inkling of what or where home is. Others sit in a daze. Some speak. Many cannot. Mostly, residents are shells of what they once were.

Still, I saw glimmers of their personalities and hints of what lay in the depths of their souls. These discoveries were the source of the gifts. But the ultimate gift was of my own making: For most of my life I had remained slightly detached. Care for my mother required a face-on commitment to love. In a new and powerful way, I experienced the fullness of becoming more human.

This is why caring for my mother began as a burden but ended as a blessing. If you are in a similar journey, I hope these gifts I uncovered can become your gifts.

INTRODUCTION

New to Alzheimer's? Why
THIS BOOK MIGHT HELP

IF someone you love has just been diagnosed with extreme dementia or Alzheimer's, chances are good that you are in shock. And that is where you should be. Your world has been turned inside out.

If you are like I was, your heart aches because you know there is no cure and the disease is progressive. Your loved one cannot go back to life the way it was, nor can you, as a guardian or caregiver.

Early clues

In mom's case, there were indications that her memory was fading, but I wanted to ignore them and pretend her life was normal. She put post-it notes everywhere to remind her where things were. She began to accuse others of stealing, but in fact she had forgotten or misplaced items. Once she drove to the mall and couldn't remember how to drive home. Imagine her own private fear and confusion during this transition. To us, she denied any problem. She wanted her life to remain as it was.

Another first sign of her Alzheimer's, coupled with memory loss, was irrational anger. Mom grew angrier every day, and she took it out on her husband Edgar. If she couldn't find something, she yelled at him. He tried to calm her down and please her, which fueled more anger. Finally, the shouting and accusations of stealing, plus her inability to reason, isolated them from friends and ultimately became too much for Edgar to handle. He started to feel like he was taking care of an infant. He felt trapped. He dared not leave mom alone.

Edgar was in his 80s, and asked me for help. That is when I became fully engaged, because I knew that I was my mother's legal guardian and, well, she was my mother! After many family discussions, we decided to transport mom from her home in Arizona to a care facility in Minneapolis, where I could more closely monitor her care and her medical needs, while including her in our family events to help her feel somewhat normal. We were doing the difficult thing of separating husband and wife.

I was ignorant about the disease and unprepared

From the start, I knew little about the disease and how to be helpful. My first shock was to find out how expensive it would be to place mom in a care facility. Next, I had the vague idea that I needed to explore legal issues around making health care and legal decisions. The issues seemed to cascade: Did I need to consider different living arrangements for her spouse?

While important, these decisions were not what was hitting me hardest: I was facing a personal loss, not only in the loss of personality and memory of the person affected, but the gradual loss of mom's part of our shared history and thus the very foundations of my relationship with my mother. Everything was shifting, fast, and answers were difficult to find.

At times, I was angry. I had to tolerate periods of indecision. I resented how this changed my life. I had to endure excruciatingly painful times of helplessness. Some days, I wanted to run away.

Although I am (I think) a clear-headed realist, I had to find ways to live comfortably in mom's increasingly absurd reality. I learned to pretend, to live in the presence of her distorted reality, because it was the only way to be at her side.

Meanwhile, the overriding shock I felt was the shock of the eraser, hanging over mom, moving back and forth, like a sharp scythe, cutting away the past and the future. Like a pendulum, each swipe and each day the disease erased in degrees the very person I loved. The irony is that I, not mom (who soon was not aware of what was happening to her), was the one to bear the extended grief.

Shock led me to an ultimate terror, which is that

I couldn't stop the progression of the disease, no matter how much I wanted to. I was now parent to my parent.

You may experience all of these transitions and feelings. They are normal.

And then the gifts began to appear

Out of this difficult situation, the gifts to me slowly began to appear. The darkness slowly lightened. The more I immersed myself in mom's life, I began to experience, of all unexpected things, joy and gratitude. It began, perhaps, when I saw my own strength in all that I had done. In facing Alzheimer's in a love one, I found out the stuff I was made of. I stared down doubts; I embraced faith. Through these gifts, I gained the strength to face death of a loved one in slow motion.

My biggest gift, besides those listed, was this: All my life I had maintained a slight detachment from that which happened around me. This experience forced me to jump in with both feet. I made a commitment to love and care for my mother, no matter how difficult it might be. Through this process, quite simply, I became more fully human.

But at this point of your own experience, you may still be in shock. And that is why this book might be just the thing you need.

Mother's Life Before the Disease

I want to share something about her so that you will perhaps better understand how the disease of Alzheimer's slowly and persistently erased so much (but not all) of her. It can do the same to your loved one.

My mother Shirley, as the saying goes, was a pistol.

Shirley was born in Duluth, Minnesota in 1922 to Harry and Dora Litman. She was the second child and first girl. Her older brother had died at birth. He is buried in the old Jewish cemetery, close to the fence, beneath a small and fading stone labeled, simply, "Baby Litman." Shirley was followed by a younger brother.

By tradition, women of this time — not all of them but most of them — often were housewives and, if they did work, had jobs secondary to their husband's. The attitude toward marriage was that "if you made your bed, you slept in it." Divorce was not common or respectable.

But there was nothing traditional about Shirley's life, from the start. Her mother Dora was a superstitious, gossipy, complaining and incredibly humorous woman. Dora had been struck by lightning when she, Dora, was a little girl, which Dora claimed endowed psychic powers. As an adult, Dora became a notorious and successful fortune teller, holding séances, Ouija board sessions, card and palm readings, mainly for the wealthy "East-Enders" of Duluth's lumber and mining families, as well as for the equally financially successful prostitutes from brothels in Superior, Wisconsin.

By contrast, her father Harry wore a suit, vest and tie every day of his life, including weekends at home.

Beauty, smarts and determination at a young age

Fashion and beauty were essential to Shirley from a young age, decidedly in reaction to her mother, who often remained dressed in her nightgown day and night. The only ornaments on Dora's nightgown were burn holes from a cigarette perpetually dangling from Dora's lips. Shirley was determined to have a more respectable life, and decided early that using her beauty, personality and nice clothes would be essential leverages.

But Shirley's determination was not just focused on the superficial. She was intent on applying her quick wit and intelligence to her advancement. To start things off, Shirley applied herself in Girl Scouts, becoming one of Minnesota's first Golden Eaglets, equivalent to an Eagle Scout. The award was pinned on her Girl Scout sash in 1937 by Eleanor Roosevelt at a ceremony in Chicago, when Shirley was 15 years old.

In high school, Shirley bloomed. She made friends and became class treasurer. She began dating the class president, Leonard Naymark, and they led the Prom dances for three years straight. At age 18, Shirley and Leonard drove to Bessemer, Michigan, and signed a marriage license.

The marriage produced four children and a boatload of stress and arguments. Still, Shirley and Leonard remained married nearly 40 years because that is what unhappy people did in those days.

Shirley had not been a warm mother. She had been practical and responsible, but not kind and loving, at least to me as I remember it. Part of her being a pistol is that she firmly ascribed to the notion that if she should suffer, everybody around her should suffer, only more. Home life was not happy.

Shirley was proud of being Jewish. She made no apologies to a world full of anti-Semitism, nowhere more intense than in Duluth. Her attitude was, "I am a Jew. So what? Deal with it." Minnesotans, who are rarely direct, seemed even more indirect in their intolerance. They exercised it slyly but bluntly, rarely owning up to it. But whenever and wherever mom uncovered it, she would go after it with a frypan. I loved her for that.

Once we children were school age, mom began working in our father's talent business. She managed the ticket office, and the business grew to be a national booking agency of big-name talent.

Meanwhile, Shirley's unhappy marriage and unhappy spirit finally wore her down. By her late 40s, she was lost, pulled between a traditional obligation to her husband and a personal obligation, deeply suppressed within her, to live her life to the fullest as the once fun, beautiful, smart and engaging person she had been. Surprisingly, from this cauldron of confusion, frustration, desperation and anger came some good things for Shirley. In fact, she was to become one of the first "liberated" women of her time.

She enjoys a renaissance

She began to redeem her life by becoming a volunteer working with juvenile delinquents. Through this experience, mom saw, and saw clearly, for the first time, herself. She, like them, was out of control, angry and thinking that the world owed her something. By mom's estimation, the world owed her happiness, fame, attention, wealth and appreciation. The world wasn't delivering. The delinquents felt the same way. Shirley connected. She had some of her first honest conversations with these delinquents, and they loved her. She was vulnerable to them, and these delinquents for the first time saw that an adult had their same anxieties. They healed each other.

The volunteer work intensified, and then Shirley, at age 51, enrolled in college. Shirley saw that drug dependency played such a role in juvenile delinquency, so she declared a major in chemical dependency counseling. In four years Shirley, at age 55, had a degree. People her age were not getting college degrees. She was a pioneer.

Shirley got jobs at large health care organizations, where she thrived. They saw her passion. They didn't care about her age. She had been reborn. Then, at age 57, Shirley started her own business, in chemical dependency counseling. How many people, let alone women, started their first business at age 57 in 1979? I was immensely proud of her.

Although she lived separately now from Leonard, Shirley was one year short of being married for 40 years. Leonard wanted a traditional wife who stayed home. He was not interested in women's liberation. There was no reconciliation. Shirley got a divorce.

Two years later, at age 59, she met Edgar, a woodshop manager who had grown up in Latvia. They married. At age 65, Shirley and Edgar retired and moved to Phoenix where they both found much happiness. Twenty years later, Shirley began to show signs of Alzheimer's, at age 85. She was admitted to an Alzheimer's care center in 2007 and lived with the disease until late 2015. She became blind the last three years of her life.

But nothing, not even Alzheimer's, erased the

fact that Shirley was a grand and powerful woman. She was a foot soldier in the evolution of women in America.

In the course of writing this book, I have asked myself many times why I remained so loyal to mom during her long and emotionally draining illness of Alzheimer's. The answer is not simple. The best I can say is that I sensed her vulnerability and understood her insecurity. I felt I owed her something for all of that. It triggered in me a son's natural protective feelings toward his mother. In caring for her, in fact, I finally and fully matured, embracing life's humilities and shedding the last, I hope, of my selfishness. To my dying day, I will believe this was part of her plan for me. She never stopped being a mother, and in her illness she was in many ways sincerer and more vulnerable and more loving, than when she had been independent.

By knowing this brief history about my mother, you may better be able to appreciate all that was taken away by Alzheimer's, and, more important, all that was untouchable by Alzheimer's and remained intact to the very day she died. Perhaps this book will prepare you for a similar enriching experience with your loved one. That is my hope.

27 GIFTS IN THE COURSE OF MY MOTHER'S JOURNEY

ONSET OF THE DISEASE, AND ENTERING A CARE CENTER

1

The gift of fear

"We must travel in the direction of our fears."
— John Berryman

About this gift

When mom displayed the more extreme behaviors related to memory loss, such as anger and irrationality, I resisted the truth of what was happening. She persisted, and her behavior frightened us. This fear was the gift of an early warning sign, and a cry for help that I needed to acknowledge before I could be helpful.

I DID not want to face the truth about mom's growing memory loss and the increasing inability of her husband to care for her in their home. I wanted to pretend her behaviors were just normal aging.

The reason I was in denial was because I was afraid. I was afraid of mom becoming unable to live independently. I was afraid that this could harm her marriage. I was afraid that I would not have the courage and skill to engage and help. I was afraid that she would become a burden to me, and I was ashamed of my own feelings of selfishness.

As mom's condition deteriorated, and as her husband cried out louder and louder for help, I became nearly paralyzed by fear.

Meanwhile, mom grew angrier and her behavior became explosive. She yelled, screamed and threw things. She accused Edgar of lying and stealing. But this anger was partly an expression of her own fear. Edgar, her husband, also was afraid. He feared that he no longer could care for mom. He feared that he was deficient as a husband. He feared that the stress of living with mom would lead to a deterioration of his own health.

Fear compounded fear. Mom kept crying for help in the twisted way allowed by her disease. She would not give up, because she could not run away from her disease, as much as I tried to live in denial.

It is hard to think of fear as a gift, but as the situation deteriorated, and my fear kept building, finally the fear broke though me, and motivated me to face mom's reality. She needed care and her husband could no longer provide the level of care she needed. My fear, ultimately, became a gift that focused my attention and resources and caused me to act.

When I could use the energy of fear as a motivation to learn about Alzheimer's, explore care options and force a dialogue with Edgar and my siblings, I was beginning to be helpful.

Alzheimer's can advance quickly, and the impact on family can be terrifying. But my fear began to dissipate once I admitted that mom had Alzheimer's. This gift of clarity is what casts aside the fear, procrastination and denial, and began a process of reconciliation to reality and my seeking of remedies.

2

The gift of self-respect

"Self-confidence is the first requisite to great undertakings."

— Samuel Johnson

About this gift

Finding family consensus can be one of the most difficult parts of caring for a parent, as I was to learn over the eight and a half years that mom had Alzheimer's. Through patience, I learned that, in my case, I must trust my own decisions. This growing self-reliance led to the gift of self-respect.

I have three sisters. I am the third youngest child. But when mom was in her 50s, she appointed me her guardian.

In this role, as mom's health rapidly deteriorated, it was my responsibility as her guardian to seek the advice of her husband and daughters and hope for consensus on how we should care for mom. Yet, ultimately, decisions were my responsibility.

Naively, I expected gratitude for my role and responsibility, and trust that I would do my best.

Instead I found conflict. The conflict was heightened by the intensity and speed with which Alzheimer's was reshaping mom and the need for major decisions in a short time.

The decisions abounded: Was she ready to be placed in a care center, away from her husband? In what state (Arizona, California or Minnesota) should her care center be? What could we afford? Should mom be medicated during her fits of anger? How should we make end-of-life decisions and what should they be?

While I was unsure of answers, my siblings had immediate opinions as to the "correct" course ahead. There was no agreement, even among them. I grew exasperated and frustrated. Edgar continued to plead for help and action. He began to lose weight and was increasingly despondent. I worried for his health and ability to remain independent himself.

I prayed for patience, but also for the strength to find my own voice. Mom's illness and this stress was beginning to heal something inside of me — an overabundance of self-doubt was giving way to inner strength and self-respect.

I had spent so much of my life deferring to others and letting others define me. What self-respect I had was hidden deep inside of me. In fact, I purposely kept it hidden to protect it. But now, during this family trauma, that still, small voice inside, the voice that knew what was best, the voice that was authentically me, the voice that reflected my voice and my wisdom, was yearning to be heard.

Slowly, I began to make decisions on my own, as mom had asked of me by appointing me as her guardian. With guidance from Edgar, I made a decision to move mom to my city. With my wife Joan's guidance, I picked a care center. I made her financial decisions and augmented her financial means with my own when necessary. With guidance from the care facility nurses, I made decisions on necessary and unnecessary medications. With advice from the care center's social workers and hospice nurses, I made end of life care decisions. I made a decision to disengage from my sister's critiques (the hardest for me of all these decisions). In short, for the first time in my life I grabbed my self-respect fully.

Then it occurred to me that this gift of self-respect was, ironically, given to me by mom because of her extreme illness, and I wondered if it had been almost some sort of plan of hers back when she appointed me her guardian, to use her eventual illness as a pretext to give me what I needed most in order to become a better human being — the gift of self-respect.

In this important and significant way, she parented me to the very end.

3

The gift of music

"Don't play what's there. Play what's not there."
— Miles Davis

About this gift

Music resides in an area of the brain almost immune from Alzheimer's. The most memory-deprived residents can access the gift of music, as singers or players of instruments. Music was a constant in mom's life, and music remained with her during her Alzheimer's. Music ushered mom into her care facility and helped sustain her, and me, through many a time of doubt and trial.

When I placed mom into her care facility, I was not prepared to be among residents who were much advanced in the disease. Their physical and emotional deterioration frightened me, partly because I had not seen Alzheimer's residents before, and partly because they foretold where mom was headed as the disease advanced.

But then, to help me (and mom) through this transition, came the gift of music. This began with frequent visits by the music therapist and her portable electronic keyboard. She was a small, thin woman with oversized kindness and cheer and a gigantic, irrepressible and contagious optimism. All the residents, regardless of their mental or physical deterioration, sang at the top of their lungs. They loved to sing. Music brought them together and into the moment. Through music, they could share something beautiful and feel like they were normal again.

One night, early in mom's stay, we sat awkwardly in a common area, across from an old, thickly varnished piano. I say "awkwardly" because mom still was not sure where she was living and why she was in a group residence, and I was not sure I had done the right thing in placing her there, feelings that were understandable because we both were so new to the disease. As I stared at the piano, I wondered who among these wandering, lost, aimless residents, all barely able to remember their own name, would be able to play the piano?

Just then an older man rolled his wheelchair up to the keyboard. His chiseled face and white shock of hair made him look like the poet Robert Frost, but he had warm, rather than flinty, blue eyes. He was tethered to his wheelchair by a cord attached from the chair to his shirt, arranged such that if he tried to get up, an alarm would sound.

The only sentence I heard this man say, while staring up at the ceiling, was, "I don't want to be late for choir practice." Mom turned to me and fretted over his predicament. She said, "We have to help him get to practice. This man conducts famous choruses that depend on him."

Suddenly, Robert Frost's hands suspended themselves above the keyboard. He paused and closed his eyes. Then his hands leapt down onto the keys, and he played a beautiful classical concerto, eyes still closed, by heart. The notes cascaded into the room, transforming the hallways into an imaginary concert hall, overtaking the institutional food smells, diminishing the diaper odors, and elevating all of us, especially the lost and vacant patients, who sat in wheelchairs or on stuffed chairs, in their pajamas, rocking back and forth to the sounds.

This gift of music once again brought us together and lifted us out of our mundane lives and worries and confusions, into momentary grace. We belonged. We were doing the right thing. All second-guessing scrambled for the exits.

The gift of music continued to attend to us throughout the rest of mom's life, in Sunday services, special concerts and music therapy. But one more particular instance stands in my memory. Some evenings on this Alzheimer's floor, my wife Joan would play the piano for the residents. Sometimes Joan played old show tunes, but mostly she played hymns, thinking in either case the residents might remember them.

They did. The residents loved the music. The

men sat quietly around the piano. Some of the women danced in their wheelchairs or even stood and flailed their arms to the music. The sight of them in their faded hospital gowns, gyrating to the music, was sometimes haunting and hideous, but also deeply beautiful.

One night, at dusk, as my wife played a favorite hymn, just beyond the window you could see the cherry trees blooming.

"When peace like a river, attendeth my way,
When sorrows like sea billows roll;
Whatever my lot, Thou hast taught me
to know,
It is well, it is well, with my soul."

The music wrapped us together, into one humanity, and washed our cares away. In all of those moments of music, I let go of my cares over mom's condition and, ushered by the gift of music, entered into moments of peace, happiness and relief. I know mom did, too.

FIRST YEAR IN THE CARE CENTER, WHEN PAST AND PRESENT MERGE

4

The gift of early memories

"The past is a work of art, free of irrelevancies and loose ends."

— Max Beerbohm

About this gift

As an antidote for the sadness of seeing my mother lose her memory, I reveled in memories of her at all stages of her life. I particularly enjoyed early memories I had of mom. These early memories were gifts that consoled me as I witnessed her journey into complete memory loss.

SOMETIMES as I sat quietly with mother in her care facility, my mind would drift back to first memories of her. They were a comfort to me.

My earliest memory of my mother was perhaps when I was three years old. The memory is of a rare summer evening in Duluth — rare because it was warm and rare because dad was home. I was on the porch swing of our next-door neighbor, Mrs. Craig, looking down the steep avenue at the front of our house. Mom sat on the cement porch, leaning into the arms of dad. Mom's skirt was pulled up above her knees and dad wore a white t-shirt. They held hands and talked in hushed tones.

Another particular early memory captures mom's personality. I may have been four years old. It was summer in Duluth, maybe late June, and we were setting the mahogany dining room table for a birthday party, probably for my sister Jean, who would be turning seven. The front door was open. A warm breeze smelling of peonies wafted through the screen door and blessed us and our little house on the hillside.

Mom turned on the record player. It was Patti Page:

> *How much is that doggie in the window? (arf. arf.)*
> *The one with the waggley tail?*
> *How much is that doggie in the window? (arf. arf.)*
> *I do hope that doggy's for sale.*

As mom cut the cake and spooned the ice cream, she faced the mirror hung on the wall above the sideboard. Her back was to us. I sat at the table, watching her look at herself in the mirror and smile as she sang along. Her auburn hair was long and wavy and soft. She danced, and her hips swayed to the music. Her lithe body was alive. She wore thick, red lipstick and smelled of lilacs. She was as delicious as the chocolate cake. I couldn't stop staring at her. She was 31 years old, already with four children, but trim and energetic and beautiful.

Fifty-four years later came Alzheimer's. Within a few years of that, mom's entire history was forgotten by her: raising children, jobs, friends, marriages, homes, struggles and victories.

But now as we sat together, I celebrated the gift of early memories. As long as I can hang onto these memories of mom, she will remain untouched and present within me, and this is a fundamental comfort.

5

The gift of holidays remembered.

"God is a comedian whose audience is afraid to laugh."

– H.L. Menken

About this gift

Alzheimer's seems to work backwards. Current memories are the first to go. The oldest memories are the last to remain. While a person might forget a husband, and even children, they will rarely forget their parents. Or holidays. Holidays are gifts of tradition that remain in the mind and provide comfort to the soul. To me they were touchpoints to a past mom and I still could share.

One cold December evening, mom and I sat in the lounge of her residence, next to a flocked Christmas tree with sparkling lights.

"Do you remember our Christmas celebrations?" I asked.

She rolled her eyes, which meant that she remembered! Why did she have that reaction? It was enough of a complication to get through Christmas in a normal Jewish family. Our family traditions went a step further, from strange to absurd, as Christmas and Hanukkah jostled for position in our home.

During our childhood, mom sought to maintain the Jewish traditions. We lit the Hanukkah menorah and sang the blessing. Dad, on the other hand tried to abandon Judaism. His parents had lost their entire family in concentration camps in Poland. Dad was convinced that Judaism abandoned him, so he abandoned Judaism. In its place, he loved the beauty of Christmas, such as the lights and songs, and he intended for our family to partake.

So we created a holiday ritual that was both inclusive and insane.

On the weekend before Hanukkah, mom set out the menorah, candles and dreidels. While she was at the grocery store buying ingredients for latkes and kugel, dad arrived home with a Christmas tree, electric lights and tinsel. Dad joined us children as we decorated the tree. Mom came home, saw the tree, and said nothing. Her silence screamed.

Monday, we went to school and dad went to work. When we came home that afternoon, the tree was gone. At dinner nobody dared speak about it, including dad. We lit the Hanukkah candles, picked at the latkes on our plates until we were dismissed to our rooms to do homework.

But we peeked out of our rooms and this is what we saw: dad got up from the table and went to the front hall coat closet. He casually opened the door and fished out the tree, which had been wedged between the coats. (Since this was an annual event, he knew where the tree would be.) A trail of tinsel marked the path where he dragged the tree out the front door and around the side of the house. He planted the tree in a snowbank in the back yard. Nothing was said.

That was our Christmas tradition. Every year I can remember, mom lit the Hanukkah candles. Dad bought the tree. While he was at work, mother stuffed the tree in the clothes closet. Dad fished it out and planted it in the back yard. Nothing was said directly, but mom and dad sniped at each other indirectly the entire holiday season.

"You used to get so mad!" I said to mom as we sat looking at the artificial tree in the common area, laughing.

"I was trying to raise you Jewish and your father was taking you out to visit Santa Claus." She laughed again.

"But you have to admit we had holiday traditions that nobody else could match," I said. "And you're laughing. You didn't used to laugh."

Memory is like that, especially memory of things long ago. It softens. It heals. It binds. Memories of holiday traditions are some of the last to go in a person with Alzheimer's, so they provided us with a common, still not forgotten, connection. For those moments of recollection, during a period when mom was drifting away, I could temporarily pull her back from the void and hold her close through the gift of holiday memories. For me, this re-affirmed our shared identity and offered temporary respite in what would become a painfully long journey into near total forgetfulness.

We had redeemed the holidays!

6

The gift of release from harmful habits

"Age is a high price to pay for maturity."
— Tom Stoppard

About this gift

People with Alzheimer's lose their memory.
Oddly, correlated with this forgetfulness is a loss
of addictive behavior. Since addictions are partly
physical, physical gratification requires reinforce-
ment from memory of that gratification. A rat
won't figure out a maze if it forgot cheese once
was at the end. I can't fully explain it, but I
noticed that Alzheimer's residents were freed
from harmful habits.

Of the hundreds of Alzheimer's residents I met, none mentioned having smoked or drunk alcohol, or seemed to miss it. Nor did I see food obsessions or hoarding or any even remotely addictive behavior. (I saw repetitive behavior, but not addictive behavior.)

I found this gift of release from harmful habits

both curious and, I suppose, ironic, because residents would be healthier and live longer in their states of memory loss. And the longer they lived, the greater the humiliations they faced: forgetting how to dress, toilet, walk, feed themselves and, eventually, even how to swallow. Yet they lived on, partly because they had shed life shortening bad habits.

For most of her life, mom had been addicted to nicotine. Mom began smoking in her 20s and quit in her 60s. For forty years, she not only smoked, she chain smoked.

Because of Alzheimer's, mom didn't recall being a chain smoker (Chesterfield, Kent, Viceroy, Carlton, Pall Mall), but her smoking had defined our lives in so many ways. From morning until night, the house was blue with smoke. The windows had a milky-white sheen. On nearly every table were porcelain cigarette lighters, cigarette holders and ashtrays. I could not picture mom except with a cigarette in her mouth.

Resentful of nearly chronic sore throats as a child, I retaliated by going to a hobby shop and purchasing small explosives, called cigarette loads. They looked like short, miniature toothpicks. I buried them in random cigarettes around the house. When mom lit one, the cigarette exploded. And so did mom's anger. Her anger was a small price to pay for my first feelings of empowerment.

Of the many movie stars mom met in the family talent business (mom ran the ticket office and dad booked the shows around the country), none was a better smoking buddy for her than Lee Liberace, an actor and pianist known for gaudy outfits and flamboyant behavior. After performances, they gabbed for hours at late dinners and smoked and smoked.

Every Christmas, they exchanged gifts, and Liberace's holiday gifts always related to cigarettes. Mom had little desktop grand pianos that played a tune and then opened to display a row of cigarettes. She had candelabra cigarette lighters. She had wind-up music boxes that doubled as cigarette holders and played "As Time Goes By" or "Claire de Lune."

While yelling at me after a cigarette exploded in her face, she would remind me that I was responsible for her addiction. During her third pregnancy (me) she was particularly anxious. To calm her nerves, her pediatrician recommended that she begin smoking.

Cigarettes were more than a habit with mom. They were a family trait. Her mother had a cigarette dangling from her mouth with an inch-long ash that flicked off as she spoke. All grandmother's prepared food had cigarette ash as an ingredient. Mother's father, a liquor salesman, smoked Camel Unfiltered cigarettes all day, even after surgeries for lip cancers. Eventually, he died of Alzheimer's too. And, curiously (and to further prove my point), he died a non-smoker because he forgot he smoked.

Neither mom nor any of the Alzheimer's

residents mentioned smoking. The habit had disappeared. This gift of release from bad habits was just part (but perhaps an important part) of how the disease simplified their lives, and in an odd way purified their body and soul, until these residents were as innocent and helpless as babies.

Here, for me, was the good news from this gift of release from bad habits: whatever anxiety, shame, fear or physical dependence was behind the habits, had been released, making the residents, and my mother, more present (but a foggy presence) and less defensive. All artifice, even the artifice of addiction, disappeared. This vulnerability made them more loveable, which is partly why my love for mom increased over the years I cared for her.

7

The gift of her unexpected presence

"Such as we are made of, such we be."

– Shakespeare

About this gift

Just when I despaired most at mom's lost memory and personality, and another round of grief was about to set in for me, she would surprise me with the gift of sudden, temporary and incredible presence, insight and wisdom. These moments came as a gift of unexpected presence and soon were gone, but I always looked forward to these unpredictable but astonishing windows into who she once was. Even Alzheimer's could not fully erase what mom was made of.

Early in her stay in memory care, mom remained capable of answering general questions, as long as they didn't require memory of a particular time or place or relationship. I began to view myself as an explorer in a new world — the new world of Alzheimer's. I catalogued what I observed and looked for patterns. I sought familiarity and predictability. I wanted to figure it out.

Just at the time I thought I had an understanding of what appeared to be a consistent downward pattern, mom would show a flash of memory or insight or humor, all of which illuminated like lightening the rich and beautiful landscape that once was her.

On one such visit, we sat together talking about her marriages.

"Mom, I've noticed that many women reach a certain age where they don't want to re-marry. Why is that?"

I really didn't expect much of an answer. I was filling time. Usually mom would answer these sorts of questions with a common response, like "Who cares?"

Instead, she displayed a moment of clarity and presence: "When you first marry a man, they treat you like a partner, and they romance you. But over time, they expect to be taken care of. It's almost like they try to train you to become their mother. Pretty soon you realize you're taking their mother's place."

"I hope my generation is different," I said.

"Don't count on it. Men expect to be served," mom said. "It's not fair, but that's the way it is. By my age, women grow tired of it."

"Do you think other women would agree with you?"

"Yes, but they might not say it."

"Why not?"

"Most women play the game. It keeps the world going. But the resentment builds until they tire of it. The men never catch on."

"Quite a point of view!"

"Yup. I could write a book. But if the secret were out, a lot of women might jump down my throat. Who needs that?" And then mom stared at nothing in particular, and was lost again and quiet.

This sudden coherence was the first from mom in weeks. It came as a surprise because at this point in her illness, mom was sinking into confusion. She could not understand a map of the United States. She couldn't work a television remote control. She believed she still drove a car and that it was parked outside, neither of which was true. She did not know the year we lived in or even where she was living.

For years to come, it would be characteristic of my visits with mom that on occasion she would suddenly surprise me with thought, coherence and opinion. These rare flashes were unforeseen, but persistent.

This gift of unexpected presence brought me comfort and joy until the day mom died. Each helped me know in my heart that I never really lost her.

8

The gift of gumption

"The guts carry the feet."

– Cervantes

About this gift

When first placed in Alzheimer's care, mom was angry. She hit the caregivers. While many with Alzheimer's show anger during the early stage of the disease, mom's anger was intense. She nearly was asked to leave the residence. This was potentially a big problem. When I came to understand that her hitting was about still wanting to be responsible for her life, I could be compassionate, and I was better able to help find solutions. It also helped when I recalled the bright side of her anger: the lifelong gift of mom's gumption.

All her life, anger was one of my mother's biggest personality characteristics and also motivators, for good or ill. And as an expression of her anger, mom hit.

Actually, that is an understatement. She walloped. Especially when she was confused or perceived to be wronged or misunderstood. Her open palms struck like cobras. She hit all of her children, and she hit us in the face. I developed facial tics from her swats, and the ticks lasted several years.

Mom's hitting behavior returned in the early days of her Alzheimer's. Mom tried to hit an aide if, in her jumbled Alzheimer's mind, she felt threatened. If a care giver tried to get mom dressed in the morning before she wanted to get up, or insisted that she take her medication, mom struck. Some caregivers refused to work with her.

Mom's hitting was not her most admirable trait, but it was related to her most admirable trait: a feisty sense of right. It was related to her gumption.

Once, at age 10, I was rummaging through boxes of old family keepsakes and I found one of the best examples of mom's feisty sense of right. It was a letter to the editor, published in the Duluth News Tribune, six years earlier, when I was four years old:

"This past summer, we took advantage of our new AAA auto club membership and drove up to their recreation place on Pike Lake. There, at the gate, we were met by a man in a white pith helmet who came out of a little guard house. He held our card up to a list on a clipboard. We would not be allowed inside, he said. I asked him what list he was looking at, since we had paid for

our membership. Our card wasn't expired. He wouldn't answer my question.

"I drove home and was hurt and furious. My daughter, sitting in the back seat of the car, disappointed at not getting to swim, was crying. I called the AAA office and asked them what possible list could have our name on it. The lady said it was a list of families that belonged to synagogues in Duluth.

"My husband fought in World War II to rid the world of Nazi hatred, particularly against Jews. As a member of the Army Air Force, he was awarded the Distinguished Flying Cross for bravery. And now we are treated as second-class citizens in our hometown in America, forbidden to sit by the lake with non-Jewish families.

"We may have won the war in Germany, but when will we win the war in Duluth?"

The letter was signed by my mother. Several months after the letter was published, the ban was lifted.

After reading the letter, I asked mom whatever happened to the old man in the pith helmet. "He died," she said. "For his sake, I hope there wasn't an angel waiting at the Pearly Gates, wearing a pith helmet and holding a clipboard, because that man's name wouldn't have been on the list of who could pass."

Mom's gumption got her out of a difficult marriage. Mom's gumption got her back to college when she was twice the age of most students. Mom's gumption led to her starting her own business and remarrying.

With this perspective of my mother, I was able to forgive her hitting and to interpret her anger as an aspect of her gift of gumption. When I explained mom's history and past anger to the nurses, they figured out a way to calm mom during her transition into residential care.

By reframing her anger into the positive concept of gumption, I could be loving, patient and helpful, instead of frustrated and dismissive. In Alzheimer's, mom's gift of gumption was another way of her saying that she still mattered, that she wanted some sense of control over her life and that she demanded to be heard.

Mom's gumption was a gift to me in all the ways that I am learning to incorporate her gumption into my own personality, especially because I am more private, deferential (and hesitant) by nature. Her gift of gumption, internalized in me, kept me from ducking my responsibilities as her son. As I participated in her care, remained at her side and advocated for her best interests, I practiced doing the same for myself.

9

The gift of a peaceful haven

"I have no past, nor have I a future."
— Khalil Gibran

About this gift

Alzheimer's residents are deeply confused and alienated from their past and present. The future does not exist. The real world becomes alien. Knowing this, the care center creates an alternative reality, a peaceful haven, which tries to mimic normalcy, while limiting the distractions of the "real" world, distractions that would cause anxiety. The gift of this peaceful haven is that it provides comfort and a structure for the new normalcy of living without a memory, and is a welcome refuge for visitors.

Within the walls of the care center, there is no past or future. Time stops. Reality dissolves. There is only the moment at hand and the unvarying routines of the day, knowing each moment is forgotten immediately.

Instinctively, I suppose, I recoiled from this new world, because it was not my world. Over time, I came to appreciate and understand how the sanctuary world served the residents.

I learned to join them in their reality, which often had no relation to the outer world. Decorations were nostalgic. Travel was unnecessary (doctors, dentists and therapists came to the care center). Routines around meals and crafts were based on comfort and on lessening anxiety.

Within this environment, mom's reality still changed from moment to moment, as she responded to an ever-changing concoction of anything that passed before her: a fragment of hallway conversation between nurses, jumbled together with something said on the television set in the common room, combined with a phrase repeated (over and over again) by a resident sitting next to her.

There is no reason to try to sort it out, because as soon as something is said, true or false, it is forgotten. These residents won't remember that they made up something. They are just trying to speak because that is what normal people do.

Their routines also help them feel normal. Most of the women get their hair fixed once a week; some get their nails polished. Within a minute of leaving the onsite salon, they forget having been there. But for the moment of being in the salon, they feel normal, because there is a vague familiarity with the past.

Often the faces of memory care residents look

like masks, and their tone can be of muted expression, sometimes with no movement. They are actors who have forgotten their lines. Time means nothing to them. They may say they are bored, but can't remember being bored a moment after they say it. They say they are bored just to appear normal.

Often memory residents sit together, watching television, doing crafts or playing games like bingo. They do not look like a typical gathering of people doing these things. Memory residents have a distinctive look. Their expression seems both calm and troubled. Their eyes usually are soft and vacant, but sometimes their eyes have a searching look. Most sit quietly, showing immense patience. Yet some seem to live in constant anxiety. One woman liked to take a box of tissues and removed them one at a time and refold them on her lap. She needed to keep her hands moving to feel productive, to feel normal. But most of the women sit motionless, not knowing where they are or what to do.

All of this behavior is protected by the peaceful shadow world that tries to minimize their anxieties and help them feel as normal as possible. This was a gift to mom, but also a gift to me. Her residence became a timeless refuge for me, where I could shed all the distractions of my life and be relaxed and present to mom.

In this calm environment, we sat for hours together, sometimes without talking. Just being together through the passage of time. I hung on to each silent moment with her, knowing that she was still my mother and that her presence comforted me. Alzheimer's could not erase that.

10

The gift of finding enough money

"I don't like money actually, but it quiets my nerves."

– Joe Louis

About this gift

One of my greatest challenges was figuring out how to pay for mom's care. Mom had few assets, and the costs of care were huge. I had to be creative, resourceful and persistent. Many people (and finally the government) contributed to what was needed. While one of my greatest fears was that there wouldn't be enough money, in the end, we cobbled together a solution. Finding enough money was, indeed, a gift and a relief. We were lucky. Other families struggle more, and longer.

Caring for a person with Alzheimer's can be a costly proposition.

Even back in 2007 and 2008, when we began this journey with mom, we were in a pickle, because the annual cost of private pay Alzheimer's care was $60,000 a year. Life expectancy varies for each person with Alzheimer's. The average life expectancy after diagnosis is eight to 10 years. In some cases, however, it can be as short as three years or as long as 20 years. The average lifetime care costs were nearly $500,000. Surely that amount has increased considerably since then.

Here is how we put together a financial solution. For the first year of care, we used mom's life savings of $30,000, plus $30,000 from refinancing her condo mortgage. Immediately, we applied for county assistance to commence at the beginning of her second year of care, knowing the application process would take months.

As part of the application, we had to account for all of her assets over the past five years, since gifting was not allowed during that period. I had to prove mom was not hiding money.

County assistance was approved, but it took 15 months, leaving three months where I had to pay monthly expenses from my own resources. Mom's Social Security was turned over to the county.

Because of the aging population, county workers are stressed and overworked. They must navigate labyrinthine rules that seem sprung upon us left and right. Communication was painful and, if the stakes were not so high, perhaps humorous. To illustrate, here is a transcript from a typical call, where I asked about health insurance.

A recording asked the purpose of my call and mom's case number. I gave both. I waited 20 minutes on hold. Finally, a woman answered.

"What is the case number?" she asked. I repeated it. "Please hold," she said.

After another five minutes, a man answered. "How can I help you?"

I told him my name and said I had a question about my mother's health plan options.

"I'm not authorized to talk with you," he said.

"Why?"

"Your name isn't on the list in your mother's file."

"But I've been working with you for more than 12 months. I am the only person who has worked with you. For goodness sakes, we know each other by name. I am the legal and financial power of attorney. You have the notarized forms assigning my status."

"No we don't."

"I'm certain you must. Will you look through the documents, please?"

"Please hold," he said.

After another five minutes, he came back on the phone. "OK, I see you do have power of attorney. But we need you to fill out a form that verifies it."

"You need a form to verify a form?"

"Yes."

"OK, if you send me that form, I will complete it. But will you answer a question for me?

"Yes. What is it?"

"My mother has health coverage that is not on your county list. Since she must switch to a plan on the list, what plan do you recommend?"

"Health plans are not my area," he said. *"You have to call a different number."*

I called the second number. It was answered by a recording. "Please leave your telephone number. We do not take direct calls."

I felt fortunate to have the patience and persistence (and sense of humor) required to succeed in getting the gift of enough money for mom's care. Few people have the resources for paying the entire costs (private pay). Even with county support, my sister, wife and I still had financial obligations. We paid for non-covered items: clothes, toiletries, bedding, the beauty shop and exercise classes, among others. But with the gift of government support, soon our focus was on mom, not on finances, and for that I will be forever appreciative of the assistance we were so fortunate to obtain.

DAILY LIFE AND ROUTINE

11

The gift of religious guidance

"That which God writes on thy forehead, thou wilt come to it."

— The Koran

About this gift

I was angry at God that mom got Alzheimer's. What a cruel trick, especially if contrived, or allowed or not stopped by God! Then I remembered mom's own religious wisdom, that there was something bigger than God that ruled the course of human life. That, she believed, was Fate. God was a force for good, but Fate determined life's course. The gift of her religious beliefs gave me peace with God and strength to carry on.

I learned of mom's deepest religious belief when I was about 10 years old. It was during our regular Tuesday night time together, just her and me, when

I helped her iron clothes. I manned the sprinkling bottle: a large glass soda bottle with a special cork that had a metal top with holes in it. Like a priest with holy water, I shook the sprinkling bottle over the shirts, before mom ironed them.

And, as always during these ironing sessions, we would chat. Anything was fair game.

One Tuesday night I had a big question on my mind. "Do you believe in God?" I asked her.

Without skipping a beat or pausing as she ironed, mom said, simply, "I believe in Kismet."

"What?"

"Kismet. It means fate."

"And what does that mean?"

"It means that what happens is meant to happen."

"Who means it to happen?"

"Kismet. It's what the Persians believe. And so does Doris Day."

"I don't understand."

As she ironed, mom started singing her favorite Doris Day song:

When I was just a little girl
I asked my mother, what will I be
Will I be pretty, will I be rich
Here's what she said to me.

Que Sera, Sera,
Whatever will be, will be

The future's not ours, to see
Que Sera, Sera
What will be, will be.

I gave her a big smile. I loved to listen to mom sing. I loved to see her happy. "More!" I said. She continued to iron the shirts, and to sing.

Now I have children of my own [she smiled
and winked at me]
They ask their mother, what will I be
Will I be handsome, will I be rich
I tell them tenderly.

Que Sera, Sera,
Whatever will be, will be
The future's not ours, to see
Que Sera, Sera
What will be, will be.

On those rare occasions when mom was a truly happy person, I loved her deeply. During our mostly stressful, sad and tumultuous home life, these precious moments were interludes of unexpected grace. Before my eyes, mom transformed into a movie star, swaying her beautiful body, singing in a happy voice, just like Doris Day. I glimpsed what she could have been, had her Kismet been better for her.

She finished the song and became silent. I heard her sigh, and then there was just the sound of the heavy weight of the iron pressing down and moving back and forth across the creaky ironing board. I sprinkled another shirt and handed it to her, for the first time looking into her eyes.

Tears welled there.

"Are you O.K.?" I asked.

She sniffed. "Sure. It's just that sometimes what will be is not what we might want. It's Fate. Don't fight it. Accept it."

I pressed on with my child logic. "Suppose you and I are crossing the street. You see a car coming fast, about to hit me. Do you let that happen, or push me out of the way?"

"Push you out of the way, if I can. But if I can't, it was meant to be."

"Where is God in all this?"

"Watching. Loving."

"So if Fate has this great plan for us, all worked out ahead of time, what is it leading to? What is the point of it?"

She ironed one of her white blouses another few minutes, deep in thought, and then said, simply, "That's the darndest thing. I don't think we ever figure that part out. We just make the best of it, and then…" She seemed to trail off in thought.

"And then what?"

She gave me a wan smile. "And then it's over."

She lifted the perfectly ironed blouse off the ironing board and gave it a satisfied inspection. "But tonight, sonny boy, tonight Kismet wants us to get this ironing finished."

And now, more than 50 years later, as I sat with her in the care center, I remembered that Kismet planned for mom to get Alzheimer's. Not God. This helped me make spiritual sense of what was happening to mom. I could be angry at Fate without giving up on God. God could work through me, if I was watching and loving, as mom said. Her gift of religious guidance gave me deep comfort and a way forward.

12

The gift of preparing for death through the death of others

"A man's dying is more the survivors' affair than his own."

— Charles Dickens

About this gift

In the course of mom's Alzheimer's, her husband, Edgar died of cancer. Through the muddle of her Alzheimer's confusion, mom could not grasp it. But for the rest of us, the unwavering courage with which he lived his life and the gallant way he accepted death were gifts to us who grieved him. His death prepared us for mom's death, years later. All death prepares us, ultimately, for our own.

I took my mother from her care facility to Edgar's, so that she could see her husband one last time before he died of cancer.

She sat on the edge of his bed. He was conscious and connected to oxygen and a permanent catheter. She could not accept that he was dying. While denial is a natural response to grief, it also is another symptom of how Alzheimer's disconnects someone from life.

"He'll be fine," she said after the visit, as I drove her back to her care center. "He'll take me home."

But Edgar really was dying, and he was matter of fact about it. He told me he had lost 35 pounds in 35 days and weighed 130 pounds. "Does this mean I will live 130 more days?" He laughed.

Two weeks ago, he had stopped eating. It was an effort to sip water. Since Edgar had loved to gamble at casinos, dog tracks and with lotteries, a more severe indication of the end was when he no longer wanted me to buy him daily lottery tickets.

"My luck has run out," he said simply.

This was a man who hadn't had a lot of luck in his life to begin with. When he was 18 years old, growing up in Latvia, his dream was to finish school in Riga and become a botanist. Then Russia invaded Latvia. Edgar joined the resistance, fighting with Germany for his homeland. A Russian infantryman shot off Edgar's right knee. Not much luck there.

Edgar was shuttled from hospital to hospital behind the German lines and then across France. After the war, he could not return to Latvia, where his country and his home were occupied by Russians. Somehow, Edgar managed to gain sponsorship to the United States, to Minnesota. He became a bricklayer, then a welder, and finally a master woodworker at a Latvian-owned shop in Minneapolis. He married and had four children. Then he divorced. Then he met and married my mother. Now he had cancer.

Life had tired Edgar. His weariness was deep. Practicality was his salvation. With their emphasis on the individual, Americans take death hard. It's personal. Europeans such as Edgar, unlike Americans, have a multi-generational perspective on life. Each person is part of a larger odyssey whose ultimate meaning is much less visible to any one person in the chain. Death is not so personal.

A few days after his goodbye to mom, Edgar slipped into a morphine slumber. He died a few days later.

My wife and I drove to mom's assisted living room to deliver the news. Mom couldn't understand what I was saying, or didn't want to believe it. She asked me to write something in block letters in her "memory" notebook, using a thick, black magic marker. My entry was simple: "EDGAR DIED." She shook it off. His death did not fit with her Alzheimer's induced absurd thinking.

Her Alzheimer's mind was full of holes, like a sieve, and all emotions, including grief, passed through it quickly. Her inability to ache over the loss of a husband was another humiliation of Alzheimer's, another affront to her humanity.

She studied the words over and over. "I guess

that means he won't be going home with me," she said.

But for the rest of us, Edgar's death was more than the gift of his release from suffering. It was a rehearsal to help us be ready for mom's death, and eventually our own. It was the gift of preparing for death through the death of others. The more we love those who pass, the more we prepare for own.

13

The gift of unique,
but familiar smells

"Deep experience is never peaceful."
— Henry James

About this gift

*I confess to never getting used to the smells of
the Alzheimer's floor. But I learned to tolerate
them and, in a strange way, befriend them, for
these smells were so consistent that they became a
shared bond and emblematic of our long goodbye
that stretched for nearly a decade. Even now, as
I write this, the thought of these smells takes me
immediately back to mom's side.*

The smells in the memory care wing of the care
center were powerful, distinctive, consistent,
memorable and repulsive. Every time the elevator
door opened on the floor, the smells assaulted me.
At the same time, I was embarrassed that the smells
mattered at all. They were the smells of old people,
of diminished capacity and of decay. But also the
smells of lingering life. Inwardly, I felt petty to even
dwell on them.

At the same time, these smells defined a large part of the experience of caring for mom during her illness. Like the taste of Proust's madeleine cakes, which unlocked sweet remembrances of his mother, the smells of the memory care floor will for me always be associated with love for mom.

They were not pleasant smells, nor were they singular. The smells were a mush of vomit, feces, diaper perfumes, stale food, body odor, various skin creams, cough drops, and cleaning solutions. This amalgam is distinct to memory care centers and, to a degree, also to almost any nursing home. The smell is so common, there must be a name for it. At times it is so strong, I learned to breathe first through my mouth, and then slowly to start using my nostrils, so as to carefully get used to it.

One whiff of that smell, even to this day, just pulled from my memory, and I see in my mind's eye, mother patiently sitting in her wheelchair, at a table in the dining/social hall, where she ate and often sat for hours between meals. The dining hall doubled as the community room, where staff delivered music therapy, spiritual conversations, memory games and stories and some exercise programs. Mother sat there in her wheelchair most of the day, except when carted off to the beauty shop or the wellness (activity) center, or brought into her bathroom for a diaper change. It was her home within a home.

One whiff, and I recall the endless days of visits,

during which I wheeled mother along the hallways, each with a window at the far end, where we would pause and I would describe the weather or the season. Mother, blind the last three years of her life, would concentrate and try to understand what I was saying.

One whiff, and I feel a surprising nostalgia for those days of sitting with her, massaging her shoulders or kissing her forehead. Even toward the end, when she had so few language skills, she would say as I tugged at her shoulders, "Mmmm, that feels good."

One whiff, and I see the other residents, mostly in wheelchairs, with blank or trouble looks, expressing confusion and loss. Some smiled at me, hoping I was there to see them, and that I would take them "home." Others hunched in their chairs, chin on chest, and slept. Still others stared straight ahead, with a patience that befuddled me. A few hardy ones still walked the hallways with walkers, asking me where they should go.

Even the thought of one whiff fills me with both a deep sadness and abundant appreciation for the eight and a half years I had with mom in some form that was not mom but was mom still. That pungent odor of the care center is a gift that will forever be easily recalled and serve as a shortcut to accessing mom's presence and love.

14

The gift of friendship

"Without friends, no one would choose to live,
though he had all other goods."

— Aristotle

About this gift

Without the ability to remember, those with
Alzheimer's become isolated from family and
even from those they live with in care centers.
But not always. This gift celebrates the excep-
tion: when two people with Alzheimer's bonded
as friends, as sidekicks. And in the way that
mother befriended the care staff. It was a gift by
which I saw that true friendship goes much deeper
than memory of shared events or complementary
personalities. Friendship has components we can't
fully understand, which is why friendship is so
precious.

Mostly, Alzheimer's residents spoke only to the aides, not to each other. During activities, they were like small children at parallel play, valuing the attention of the teacher alone. At meals, the only interaction between residents that I saw was an occasional nasty word or threatening gesture, usually in reaction to a misunderstanding from words said in unconscious babble.

Except for family visits, Alzheimer's residents lived as they died, alone. In this way, Alzheimer's made friendships among peers difficult and uncommon, but not impossible, and always to be recognized and celebrated.

Why were friendships difficult? First, memory loss made it hard for residents to remember the people they lived with and sat next to. The confusion was made more difficult because of constant population churn. I saw firsthand that as current residents died and new ones arrived, mom's social group changed regularly and frequently. A dying memory did another terrible thing that hindered friendship: it turned the most gregarious person inward. Residents became like children, focused on their needs in the moment, rather than showing interest in others.

Still, in eight years of mom's disease, I saw touching exceptions of resident-to-resident friendship. For example, there was the friendship between residents Ruth and Donna.

Both women, in their late 80s, came to the care center about the same time. Ruth had a sweet face with frightened blue eyes. Her entire nature was timid. She had forgotten much about herself except that she wanted dearly to belong. To counter that, her favorite response was "Me, too." If someone said they liked a certain food or television show, Ruth said, "Me, too." If someone said her daughter was mean to her, Ruth said, "Me, too." She did not know where her room was. She was terrified to be alone. In this way she was like Ruth in the Bible, saying wherever you go, I shall go.

Donna, on the other hand, appeared to have been a refined person, highly educated, who said she once owned a small dress shop. Even now, she wore beautiful outfits. Donna had more wits about her than most residents. She walked without a walker, itself a symbol of higher overall functioning.

Almost immediately, for reasons unknown, Ruth and Donna sought each other out and became inseparable friends. Ruth followed Donna down the hallways. Ruth was sure to sit next to Donna at meals or activities. In no time, Donna took it upon herself to harbor Ruth. Many nights after aides dressed the residents in their pajamas and tucked them into their beds, Ruth's door would slowly open. Ruth would edge her face through the door crack and shyly peer up and down the hallway. Then she would emerge, like a hermit crab, almost in slow motion, and quietly shut her door behind her. In the dimly lit hall, as lost and disoriented as Ruth was, she found her way to Donna's room, opened the door and slipped in. There she gently edged herself onto Donna's bed and soon there she slept, huddled close to Donna.

Ruth was afraid of the night, just as she seemed afraid of life during the day. Donna was her comfort.

One morning, I visited the care center and found Ruth sitting alone in her room, whimpering. I asked Ruth to tell me what was wrong. "I don't know," she said.

"I'm sad to see you like this," I said.

"Me, too," she said.

Then I found out from the staff that only a day ago Donna's family had moved Donna to a different care center. Ruth's best friend had left her.

In the days that followed, Ruth preferred to remain in her room. She skipped group activities. She took her meals alone. Whenever I peeked inside, and said hello, Ruth's soft and faded blue eyes welled up with tears. "I'm alone," is all she said.

One day when I looked inside her room to say hello, I was startled to see new furniture. I asked the care staff where I could find Ruth. They looked at me and just shook their heads. Some rule or unwritten code requires that staff share no personal information on residents. Ruth had died.

The loss of her last, great friendship had made life not worth living. Mom, unlike Ruth, was gregarious, mostly with staff and not with other residents. She lit up when they greeted her or joked with her. She thrived on these friendships, and the staff delighted in being with mom. I know this helped sustain mom, just as seeing it gave me great joy. I, too, experienced the sustaining gift of friendship with mom. Yes, she was my mother, but because she was so dependent on me, I adopted yet another role to sustain both of us, and that was to be her friend.

15

The gift of dance

"Music touches places beyond our touching."
— Keith Bosley

About this gift

Lilly was my strongest proof of the triumph of the human spirit over memory loss. She refused to cede either her deepest horror or strongest joy to Alzheimer's eraser. The two conflicting emotions stubbornly co-existed in Lilly, and when she expressed them concurrently, by dancing to a tune only she heard, she seemed to seek some sort of unconscious reckoning.

Even severe Alzheimer's could not always be counted on to erase all memory, particularly a bad memory, or even certain joyful ones. These memories, like crafty children, found closets to hide in to avoid that thief called Alzheimer's, and they sprang forth, sometimes often, seeking some sort of final resolution.

I saw this in many residents, but never so strongly as in the case of Lilly.

Lilly was born in Romania in the 1920s. She grew

up in Bucharest, at the absolute wrong time: when Antonescu sided with the Nazis against the Soviets and intensified pogroms against the Jews. Lilly was a Jew.

Amid this terror, Lilly told me life must go on. She married in 1940. Due to boycotts against Jewish businesses in the commercial center, Lily and her husband and baby daughter moved back to Lilly's parents' home in the suburbs. There, the family was taunted and humiliated, and the death squads, which went house to house, visited Lilly's home like a Passover plague. Amid this carnage, and not untouched by it, somehow Lilly, her husband and daughter escaped through Europe to the United States.

Now, nearly seventy years later, Lilly was a resident in mom's care center. In Lilly's muddled mind, she thought that I was an old and dear friend with whom she could share her agonizing past.

"It was terrible," she told me as we sat in the common room one day. "Unspeakable!" She began to whimper and cry. "They brought my brother into the back yard of our home. It was a walled garden. They pushed him up against a big tree. All of us screamed, watching in horror, and the soldiers raised their guns and shot him. Dead. My own brother. As a warning to us to leave. To go anywhere."

"Can you imagine such an unspeakable thing?"

she said, looking up at me with eyes that still sought an answer.

Over the year that I knew Lilly, she repeated her story of survival to me many times. Each time she cried. Each time the story was different. Once it was her father who was pushed up against the tree and shot. Once it was her favorite cousin. In another version there was a violinist, made to play barefoot while dancing on a stage of broken glass. Scattered among all of these versions, there were dead bodies of Jews, wrapped in taluses and lined up in gutters.

"I can't tell you the horrors! They haunt my dreams," Lilly said. So deeply were these images seared in Lilly's mind, even Alzheimer's could not search out and destroy them. They were like cancer cells adept at hiding from treatment.

But there was one thing more about Lilly which completely contradicted her sad history. She loved to dance.

She danced whenever music played. She danced to silent tunes that played in her head. She danced alone. If the residents, arrayed in a circle of chairs, were watching a television show, Lilly jumped up from her chair without visible prompting, moved to the middle of the circle, and began to dance.

Because Lilly was a small woman, under five feet tall, watching her dance reminded me of the miniature ballerina atop a music box, twirling and dipping and spinning to the music.

Most curious, though, was not her dancing, but the expression of rapture on her face when she danced. She became angelic. As she spun and spun, her face would tilt toward the ceiling lights, her eyes would close and she waved her hands and arms like a flapping bird, getting ready to fly. She radiated pure joy.

Dance fought against the pain of Lilly's bitter past. Dance was her reckoning. Hate lost. Dance won.

I cannot since watch anyone dance, whether alone, as a pair or in any sort of community, without a deeper understanding of the joy it expresses and a memory of Lilly's courage. I used to think dance was about music, rhythm, joy and fun. But it also, thanks to Lilly's gift of dance, is, to me, about transcendence and freedom.

16

The gift of the care community

"The loving are the daring."

— Bayard Taylor

About this gift

The care center was staffed by hundreds of loving souls, all working together, mostly for low wages. Often, English was their second language. Yet for company and comfort, and for decency and humility, these aides excelled. They went about difficult tasks with patience and kindness. The gift of the care community was not only a gift because the aides softened mom's journey with their competence, but a gift to me. I learned humility. I was reminded that what really matters is what we do for others, not what we do for ourselves.

If you have a loved one who becomes a resident of an Alzheimer's care center, you also enter into this new society with the chance to make friends among the residents and care staff. To join in is a gift and honor.

By participating in mom's care, and being present, I joined the huge community of caregivers.

I saw most of them every visit, for days and days, and years and years. I got to learn and mimic their effective skills, by understanding their care philosophies and how they coordinated their work with each other, always for the benefit of the residents. I also befriended them and learned about their families and dreams.

The care community was huge. There were dietitians, food workers, personal attendants, nurses and nurse assistants, exercise physiologists, durable medical equipment specialists, spiritual directors, floor social workers, floor nurses, doctors, receptionists, gift shop volunteers, accounting staff, janitors, handymen, ventilation specialists, carpet cleaners, clothes labelers, pool exercise aides, beauty shop operators, manicurists, music therapists, in shifts covering the 24 hours of the day.

While some of the administrators were born and raised in the U.S, many of those who provided hands-on help were immigrants. A lot of the immigrants were from Africa. Each one I met told me much the same story. In their country, caring for the sick and elderly was expected of family. There were no institutions. So they naturally knew how to do the work.

While their daily tasks were to comfort, dress and feed the residents, the "work" often meant cleaning up vomit, wiping someone after a bowel movement and cleaning excrement from bed linens or clothing.

This they did all with professionalism and a smile, and with respect for the resident.

Even with these difficult jobs, these workers had a better life than they ever could have achieved in their home country. One told me, "Here in America there are no night visits from paramilitaries, no rape, no stealing of your things by gunpoint. Instead you can save money to send home, or use it to help your children attend college and have a better life. We are blessed to be here."

Evidence of this belief was everywhere. A former teacher from Guyana was working at the care center so he could send his second daughter to college. An aide from Liberia bought, for the first time, prescription glasses to better read the Bible. An aide from Sierra Leone was getting her registered nurse degree. An aide from Kenya proudly told me his three little boys are Americans, born here.

Most can't afford cars. To get to and from work, many stand at frigid bus stops during the long winter, for the honor of having a low-wage job, for which they are overjoyed.

While these aides helped ease mom's journey, they gave me a gift, too. Even though I am part of a country that often holds the financially successful in highest regard, I found that the care aides became my heroes among all the stratifications of our society. Watching them, imitating them and admiring them, helped me engage more fully in mom's care and even re-order my own values system by observing what truly is important in how we treat each other, more than whatever it is that we own.

17

The gift of seeing each person's essence

"There is a secret person undamaged in every individual."

— Paul Shepard

About this gift

There are plenty of aggravations and grief in having a loved one with Alzheimer's, but there also is the gift of enjoying a relationship with the inner-most part of the person you have known and loved sometimes your entire life. Gone are their profession, their relationships, their ego, their language and, of course, their memory. But an essential piece remains. The core person remains. One gift of Alzheimer's is to experience what remains, to understand its worth and uniqueness, and to wonder if that core or essence is, indeed, a peek at the person's very soul.

Those who work in Alzheimer wards across the country have articulated to me the same single-most reason for loving their job: you get to see people's unadorned self like nowhere else.

How is this the case? Simply put, memory enables artifice. Memory provides an arsenal of defenses and a wardrobe of disguises. Memory protects us. Memory is the fuel of our learned behaviors. Often, memory is used to hide what is deep inside.

It is memory that we use to anticipate contact with someone we've come to know. In certain social or work situations, we anticipate the crowd and use memory to prepare ourselves to our best advantage, which sometimes, and maybe often, includes necessary deception. We put on airs, as the saying goes. We strategize ahead of time for our best hoped-for results. We hide what we perceive as weaknesses or vulnerabilities.

Memory is like clothes. We use memory to hide behind ourselves, for it helps us anticipate what others want to see, or what we want to show. Memory helps us create and sustain a masquerade of who we really are.

Now take away memory, and the upside is that you also take away all that is false or contrived. The Alzheimer's resident has forgotten how to hide and how to dissemble. What is left and what you see is the person stripped down to their essential self.

In the case of mom, gone were the poufy hair, the makeup, the jewelry and the ditzy-play-acting. Gone were the guises that suited her in life: the fashion ingénue, the businesswoman, the helpless wife, the snarky friend, the insecure and hurt woman always looking for some endorsement, even from strangers.

Now, because of Alzheimer's, she was just Shirley, in her essence: a wounded, sometimes cantankerous, funny, clever and exasperated soul.

In an Alzheimer's care center, the essences are there to see, visible, no longer dissembling, no longer able to hide. And it is amazing to watch them.

For instance, there was Betty, who wore black gloves and a navy overcoat, inside, where the ambient temperature was already warm, always, even at dinner, because her essence was very proper, private and correct.

There was Molly, desperate to find someone she could walk behind and follow. She had been abandoned in death by two husbands, and largely ignored by daughters whom she sensed were burdened by her needs. Her essence was governed by fear of abandonment.

There was Alice, always hopeful that her son will come and take her to his home to live, knowing in a way deeper than memory that he was too busy with his own family for that to happen. Straining her sight through thick lenses, she read the real-estate ads in papers and magazines, long into the evening, after others had been put to bed, until she fell asleep at the table. Her essence was one of hope, disappointment and understanding.

There was Ruby, arguing with every tablemate over having enough space and then complaining with the cooks over the food set before her. In spite of all behaviors to the contrary, Ruby wanted to be seen as amenable, so she continually shouted, "That'll work." But nothing worked for her. Her essence was angry, particular and contrite.

The list went on. There was Mildred, who guarded her food like a wild animal, and then wolfed it down. She sat with a constant frown on her pinched face as her only companion, refusing to talk to anyone except the aides, whom she regarded as bestowing upon her the status almost of royalty. Her essence was filled with emptiness.

I suppose working with those with Alzheimer's is not unlike being a kindergarten teacher. Your students are too young to have learned serious artifice. You love them for their vulnerabilities and their humanity.

As the residents presented themselves so honestly, I was given a gift, too, not only to see them honestly and unadorned, but of being inspired to understand my own essential self. This work helped me be more authentic to the residents, because any artifice I could present to the residents was neither understood nor appreciated. I found that they responded best to honesty, kindness and presence. I could call up these traits in myself, and anything I do moving forward in life to express these particular parts of me will give me the gift of being better aligned with who I am and focused on what matters.

18

The gift of letting go of life

"Memory, of all the powers of the mind, is the most delicate and frail."

— Ben Johnson

About this gift

Mom traversed several phases of memory loss and debilitation over eight-plus years of Alzheimer's. But to characterize this as "debilitation" might not be fair, because memory loss helped mom get through these long years as if they were days. I had to remind myself that her diminished mind was not painful, embarrassing or distressing to her. It did me no good to wring my hands in despair as my mother slowly drifted away. In an ironic way, her memory loss actually was a gift in that it made her journey easier for her. She was letting go, and trying to give me the gift of letting go, too.

The progression through memory loss happens in different intervals for each resident. Memory becomes more fragile. Expression becomes more difficult. Eating becomes harder. Movement becomes more restricted. Some residents can pass through the phases in a matter of a few months. Others, like mom, moved through the stages more slowly, taking eight years for her journey.

A benchmark of the progression of mom's illness was her annual assessment by the county social worker. Each time I was present, and recorded the conversation. Here is mom at the midpoint of moving from reality and memory to, I suppose, extreme detachment from present reality.

The social worker began with a pleasantry. "This is such a nice room you have."

"It's O.K.," mom said, making a dismissive face as if to say she was accustomed to better.

"How long have you lived here?"

Mom tapped her chin with her forefinger, pondering the question. "I think I came here yesterday." (Three years, I told the social worker.)

"Do they keep you busy?"

"Not really. It's kind of boring here." (They have activities every day, as you can see from the chart on the wall, I told the social worker.)

"Do they give you your medications?"

"I don't take medications." (Her medication box is under the end table. The aides administer medications twice a day.)

"How often do you see a doctor?"

"I don't have a doctor."

("Dr. S--," I told the social worker.)

"I wouldn't know him if I saw him." (About twice a year, I told the social worker. Generally, her health has been stable.)

"Do you have many friends here?"

"Not really. I keep to myself. People aren't particularly friendly." (She chats with everybody, I said.)

"How often do you take a bath?"

"Whenever I want. There's a shower in the bathroom." (The aides bathe her once a week down the hall in a special room with a walk-in shower.)

"And how are you handling money?"

"Sometimes I let Rick get things for me." (I handle her finances, I told the social worker.)

"Do you have any concerns you'd like to discuss with me?"

Mom shook her head. "No, it doesn't matter. I'm going home tomorrow."

And so ended the assessment. Had the social worker done an annual assessment on me, she would have found that I was changing in a parallel way, but not in terms of memory as much as acceptance. Instead of anguish at mom's diminished grasp of reality, I was beginning to accept her journey and even find some pride in these exchanges. I was glad that mom still imagined she was in charge. The larger gift working on me was a relief that her memory loss was not just the cause of her debilitation, but almost a mental anesthetic to ease the journey she was on. Thinking this way lessened my sadness for mom. It was the gift of letting go, working in both of us in different ways.

19

The gift of enjoying absurdity

"There are no facts, only interpretations."
— Friedrich Nietzsche

About this gift

At first I thought that correcting mom's absurd thinking would help her stay in touch with reality. Eventually I found that approach made as much sense as assuming that logic could cure cancer. Once I was able to suspend reality, and join the absurd life in an Alzheimer's care center, this alternative universe, I ironically felt much calmer and more present. This helped me be more present with mom, so why not?! And as Ivy Compton-Burnet says, life has no plots anyway.

As Alzheimer's progresses, the conversations of the residents become more absurd. At first I was flabbergasted. But soon I came to enjoy their bizarre world, because absurd conversations were still conversations. I knew that what the future held would be much worse: a time when residents would forget how to converse at all.

Meanwhile, absurdity is a wild ride, but also a

fascinating ride, if you hang on. Just recently, Lilly came into the common room where I was sitting with mom.

Lilly looked at me and then back to mom. "Is this man your husband?"

"What?!" mom said, and then she pointed at me: "Who, him?"

"Yes," Lilly said, smiling at me. "This gentleman."

"No, he's my brother."

I corrected mom. "I'm your son."

Mom looked at me quizzically. Then she pulled three paper napkins out of her pocket. "Who should I give these to?"

Lilly pulled a napkin out of her sleeve. "Not me. I have one. See?"

"Then what am I supposed to do with these?"

Lilly pondered the question. "I don't know. Should we ask somebody?"

"Who?" mom asked.

"Your brother."

"Mom, why don't you just put them back in your pocket?"

Meanwhile, Lilly was smiling at me. Then she shocked me, by spitting three times at me. "Piff, piff, piff."

"Do you need a napkin?" Mom asked of Lilly.

"What are you talking about?"

"You were sneezing!"

"No! I am wishing this gentleman a long life."

Lilly spit at me three more times. These well-wishes were beginning to irritate me, so I said: "Let's say goodbye to Lilly, and I'll take you to your room."

"She has bad manners," mom said as we headed to her room. "You're supposed to cover your mouth when you spit. I think I have a napkin for her somewhere here."

As absurd as was this entire conversation, when I accepted it as a new normal, I felt less befuddled and more enjoyed the gift of being present. I didn't fret at the irrationality of it. After all, there was something of a conversation between mom and Lilly. Something of a human connection, even if both forgot it the instant they parted, if not before. So whether it was logical or illogical didn't matter. The gift to me was to accept the absurdity, and even to find it fascinating, like trying to assemble a puzzle with half the pieces missing.

20

The gift of faith

"All things flow, nothing abides."

— Heraclitus

About this gift

Mom's health and memory continued to deterio-rate. In spite of the awful things that happened to her, she remained patient and accepting. Her deterioration had the unexpected effect on me of increasing my love for her and strengthening our bond. I had no room for pity, only admiration at her strength and dignity. She gave me the gift of her example to remain as present as she could in the face of significant problems. She gave me the gift of faith.

As if Alzheimer's were not humiliating enough for mom, more ailments beset her and tried to bring her down, as if she were Job himself.

Already blind in her right eye, her sight began dete-riorating in her left eye, the consequence of chronic glaucoma. We tried two operations to remedy, or at least postpone, her illness, knowing that loss of sight would further reduce her connection to reality and accelerate her memory loss, isolation and decline.

The surgeries failed. Now she was blind.

Blindness required a heightened level of care. Mother needed complete assistance in dressing, toileting, getting in and out of bed and eating. Her aides stepped forward, with both a smile and laudable patience.

Mom adapted. She learned to use her fingers to place her food onto a fork and then to find her mouth with the fork. Along this journey, much dropped into her lap. Still, aides encouraged her to feed herself, however inefficiently, and then helped her finish her meal. I fed mom, too, and experienced an emotional role reversal: I imagined her once helping me, as an infant, to eat in much the same way as I was helping her now.

Mom loved chicken and rice, bananas and anything chocolate. She had always loved chocolate. Are favorite tastes separate from memory? Why do they linger?

Mom was faltering in other ways: She could not articulate a thought or finish a complete sentence. Minute by minute, she was unclear of where she was or what she should do. She needed assistance to stand up and walk just a few feet. Her strength was failing.

Fortunately, her hearing remained strong. Often, she responded with disjoint words to someone who was talking to another person, not her, because mom lacked visual clues to see she was not the intended audience.

During my visits, I sat next to her, watching her and wondering at her life, as it was now. Each moment was forgotten by her. She did as she was told, and the script she followed was simple: she was woken up, dressed and fed breakfast. She sat at music or story-telling, ate lunch, toileted, slept in the wheelchair or her bed, awakened, ate dinner, and was changed into a night gown. Then she slept the night through. In the morning, she showed wisps of personality. She recognized me by my voice, sort of. Time, though, had become circular. Redundant. Day after day, after day after day, were much the same, yet marching to an inevitable end.

My step brother said, "Shirley is trapped in life." I was sad to think of it this way, but I suppose in some manner we all are held hostage by life. We make the best of it as we are able, given our gifts and dispositions. Sitting quietly next to mom, amid her deterioration but also stubborn and placid tenacity, I had ample time to think deeply about the value of human life. It might have been easy for someone to see mom's life as expendable, now, in her current state. I could not bring myself to even harbor that judgement in my mind. I have heard arguments for assisted suicide and the right to die with dignity. To each his own, but for me, I believe the biblical command that only God, who gives life, can take a life.

Therefore, I could not pray that she should die, that God take her. I derived comfort from being with her. She personified silent, unconscious courage. There was deep wisdom inside her. She could not articulate her wisdom any more than could an elk, a tree or a mountain. But all of them are indispensable to what makes us human, and whatever that thing is, it rubs off by proximity and over time.

Since mom could not see me, I trained myself to feel our connection by standing behind her, and to bend down and encircle my arms around her arms as she sat below me in her wheelchair. I hugged her. I stroked her arms. I kissed the top of her head. I knew she liked it. I liked it. She was my mother and she was still here. I wish I could explain this experience, but any explanation I try seems to diminish the awe and gratitude I felt. We were like two animals with a common, unspoken language. She gave birth to me. I, like a seed, clung to the husk from which I had burst forth. Although she did not have the words, and I don't have the words, I knew in my heart that my safety, security and right to life derived from her, and from her alone, and the grace of God.

So even though our time together brimmed with inarticulate meaning, mom was still a resting place for my soul. Of this I was clear: When she died, I would remain tethered to others, but my life and the peace within me would never be the same. But my faith, strengthened by mom and her journey, would abide.

21

The gift of reprieve

"The butterfly counts not months but moments,
And has time enough."

— Rabindranath Tagore

About this gift

Even in mom's inevitable path toward further
deterioration of mind and body, there were
temporary reprieves. There were "good days"
or times together that were calming and precious
because time, which seemed to be whisking mom
away, took a temporary break from its headlong
pace, and stood still. Such were the times when
mom and I sat in the courtyard, under a warm
summer sun filtering through the locust trees,
connecting without need for words. Whenever
I am distraught about anything, I call up this
scene and feel the gift of reprieve — reprieve from
the loss of mom, and reprieve from the relentless
march of time.

Of all the simple but precious time I spent with
my mom, none was as sacred and delightful as
the warm summer afternoons we shared outside, in

the courtyard of her residence, sitting together under the canopy of the locust trees.

During our sojourns mom didn't have much to say. She couldn't see and her mind was not hospitable to a complete thought, let alone to voicing of it. But I think she liked the warmth of the sun on her face and the sound of the sparrows in the trees. While outside, we celebrated the rare times in our northern clime that the air was sultry. Still, I wrapped mom in double sweaters to fend off a possible chill. Without words to bind us, we sat knee to knee, so she would know I was there.

Covering the brick walls that enclosed this inner space were vines with large, grape-like leaves. Even when the leaves would die in the fall, their delicate tendrils gripped the wall against the blasting cold winds of winter. I felt a kinship with these tendrils and vines, for I was hanging on to whatever was left of mom, even as time tugged her away from me.

Like the vines, I hung on through the seasons and the years. Visiting. Caring. Handling the necessities of mom's life. She asked nothing of me. She lived mostly in silence, biding her time. Her persistence was passive, like a flowing river. The determination was all mine. Like the vines, I refused to let go.

During these soft summer afternoons, other families would wheel their feeble loved ones outside, settling at other tables and chairs, until the separate parties were arranged in a still-life promenade around the circular courtyard. Grandchildren, oblivious to the cycle of life, chased each other or played games, their parents meanwhile managing responsibilities to both generations. Some husbands who were of sound mind would read quietly to their debilitated wives. In these clumps of people, I witnessed real love, love that refused to give up for the sake of other conveniences. Love that was celebrated with modesty beneath the blue sky and warm winds, sheltered by the waving green wall of the vines and the green canopy of the locust trees.

These summer afternoons were a respite for me from so many things: from the inside disinfectant smells of the resident floors, the artificial lights, the confinement that accompanies loss of capacity, the constant worry, the sadness over undeserved fates, and my own selfish lists of things to do. Just now, we were together, brought into the common moment and equalized by the blessings of nature.

With simple joy I could sit there with mom, no words spoken, until the late afternoon chills descended and the shadows crept down the brick walls and across the soft leaves of the vines and locust trees. Mom pulled the sweaters tight around her, signaling our time to go back inside.

Inside we would go, together with all the parties, as if we were leaving a sacred church service convened informally by St. Francis in the hills of Assisi, buoyed by the gift of reprieve.

PREPARING FOR AND EXPERIENCING DEATH

22

The gift of a slow passage

"Every perfect traveler always creates the country where he travels."

— Nikos Kazantzakis

About this gift

It can take a long time to die from Alzheimer's. The pain of the slow passage to death of a loved one is about witnessing their deterioration and humiliation, time and again, and not being able to stop or reverse it. The pain becomes personal. But the gift of this slow passage is having ample time to savor the person's life and to maintain whatever relationship is possible.

IN many cases, and definitely in mom's case, death by Alzheimer's was death in slow motion. The world of the living and the world of the dead overlapped for long periods. By the time mom was 92 years old, she had one foot in this world and one foot in the next, with nearly two more years remaining before she would die.

Alzheimer's can be a long goodbye.

As I sat with her I remembered a favorite Thornton Wilder quote from *The Bridge of San Luis Rey*: "There is a land of the living and a land of the dead and the bridge is love, the only survival, the only meaning." Whatever world each of us was now in, for it seemed that we were in different worlds even as we sat together, we were connected by love.

Mom had shrunk. She was probably five feet tall, reduced by four inches. Her legs and thighs remained slender, as were her shoulders. She carried most of her weight around her waist.

Her skin was paper thin, easily torn just by brushing her arm against her wheelchair. Special cloth wraps covered her arms and lower legs to prevent skin tears or bruising. Sometimes she used these wraps to blow her nose, simply because she could not understand or remember their intended use. Her feet swelled. Her shoe size increased from 7 to 8.

In spite of the ravages of age and Alzheimer's, her face remained pretty. Her nose was straight and small. Her eyebrows, long plucked, made shallow divots in her forehead that somehow made her seem regal. She had high cheekbones. Her hair was dyed light red and sat atop her head in thin confusion. Her lips had natural color, as if she wore a light shade of lipstick, which of course she didn't. Her skin was freckled, as it always had been, since her childhood.

From time to time, she ventured to connect with the outer world. Her mouth tried to form words, but the words came out jumbled. She showed momentary frustration, but then she quickly and calmly settled into a dead end of silence.

Mom forgot her thoughts and expressions moments after she began to form them. She said things like: "What was that guy who was...." Or "When are we supposed to...." Most sentences remained unfinished.

She remembered I was her son, Rick, but recalled little else about me. For brief and unaccounted or unexpected moments, she seemed clairvoyant, saying, "I'm so confused. Nothing makes sense." Then she became distracted. This sudden reprieve from her continual state of distraction then lapsed back into oblivion. Now, even in her best moments, time and space tumbled and twisted over each other.

I pushed her wheelchair along the hallways. From time to time, I leant down and encircled her shoulders with my arms, kissing her head. Sometimes I massaged her neck and back. When I left, I promised to see her in a couple days. She simply said, "O.K. Thank you."

Then she slouched into her wheelchair, closed her eyes, and tried to sleep.

Mom deserved a better ending to life than this. That is true for all who get Alzheimer's. Perhaps to herself, at least at some level, she had died years ago. To us, she was alive by a thread, still here, representing 92 years of history and family connection.

I found that when I was with her, I could be as confused as she was about whether in so many ways she was alive or dead, and whether I was visiting her in this world or the next. But at the same time, I enjoyed the gift of her long presence and the slow goodbye. A friend once told me that he never let go of anything without leaving claw marks on it. Similarly, I hung onto mom. You only get one mother. As difficult as this slow death was on her and all of us, it was a gift that showed me the tenacity of life, the strength of love's bonds and the value of duty.

23

The gift of rebirth

"One short sleep past will wake eternally
And death shall be no more;
Death thou shalt die."

— John Donne

About this gift

For years, I thought of death as an end and
heaven as fiction to quell fear of the unknown
or to manage the transition to nothingness.
Seeing close up mom's straightforward but intense
process of dying caused me to reconsider all past
assumptions around death. Watching her steady
and unemotional process — indeed straightfor-
ward and calm process — it occurred to me that
mom was so clearly not getting ready to die, but
was getting ready to be reborn. She gave me the
gift of rebirth.

Something changed in mom when she initiated the process of dying. I had the sense that mom suddenly was on a path to leave us and the Earth, and to free herself so she could move beyond time and space as we know it, beyond the limits of her physical body, and even beyond Alzheimer's.

It was like a light switch was thrown somewhere in the dark unknown. With this new space illuminated, she was moving to the next place of being.

The start of the process was a new and distant look in her blind eyes. It was an expression of both resolve and retreat. Mom was still here, sitting in her wheelchair, but she also had begun a degree of separation. Her face was calm, devoid of expression, but resolute. Her lips were pursed and drawn tight. She stopped responding to sound, touch or smell, as if she severed the senses which had connected her to life. She was getting ready to be reborn somewhere else.

Mom was awake, but almost in a trance. I could feel her departing, even though her body was in front of me. Mom was going away.

When the nurses put her into her bed, mom's body was compliant, but unresponsive. She lay in the position she was put. She did not move on her own in an effort to increase her comfort. Her body was baggage set on a rack, ready for a trip. She was done with her earthly work.

I wanted to grab mom by the shoulders and shake some life back into her. I wanted to keep her here. I wanted to fight for her life as if I were fighting for my own. I was afraid of her death, as I might be afraid of my own. I expected her to sense my urgency. But no matter what I said or how I touched her, she was unresponsive.

She was separating from me and everything that represented her life here, and she was doing this at a deeper level than detaching through memory loss. Mom was showing me there is a time to die and that time was coming. She was accepting it without any concern. She was unemotional and at peace.

Oddly, mom now was no longer an Alzheimer's resident. She was a normal person doing a normal thing in a normal way. She was dying. Shouldn't I celebrate her return to normalcy, even if it meant letting her go?

The miracle of life is also that it has a shelf-life. Mom was ending her life here, but doing so in a matter-of-fact way that suggested confidence, not fear. It was as if she was about to be reborn. This hope made my heart happy, and also made my heart feel like it had been wrung out like an old washcloth.

But for mom, she was on her journey. The pale horse stood waiting. She all but hopped on.

24

The gift of accomplishing the great transition

"Toward the person who has died, we adopt a special attitude: something like admiration for someone who has accomplished a very difficult task."

— Sigmund Freud

About this gift

Grief and endings are painful to me. I love to say "hello." I hate to say "goodbye." I avoid it. But watching mom die over the span of seven days was awe-inspiring (and heart-breaking). My surprise gift: The process of witnessing her death convinced me she wasn't saying goodbye to life. She was saying hello to what is next, with her typical courage.

It took God seven days to create the heavens and the earth. It took mom seven days to die. Here is how the end came:

Day 1   Food became a plaything. Mom liked the texture on her fingers, as does a child. She was now sustained by chocolate drinks fortified with protein.

Day 2   Mom refused all nourishment. She was brought to the common room for four hours, during which she mostly slept. The other 20 hours, she slept in bed. She had lost 15 pounds from her normal weight.

Day 3   She remained in bed all day. Mom's entire aspect changed. If a body can express disengagement, hers did. She seemed more distant, more removed from life. She showed another level of separation from us and from life. To try to call her back seemed selfish and cruel.

Day 4   Miraculously, mom agreed to get out of bed. She went to the beauty salon and had her hair fixed, but then she returned to her room and went to sleep. The nurses suggested hospice care.

Day 5   In bed all day, mom had periods of wailing, sometimes sharp and haunting. Medication reduced her agitation. She slept.

Day 6   Medication kept her comfortable and sleeping. She no longer responded to words or touch. It was Christmas Eve. We met with Hospice during the day.

Day 7   Mom slept all day. Her breathing grew labored. She died at night. Christmas night. My wife and I were at her side.

For me, these were seven days of intense grief and helplessness. Said a friend: "You did not make her old, and you can't grant her eternal life." Sober thought. No matter how much was said in condolence, I once more was reminded that in the face of death, words always fall short.

I stood over her body in both awe and respect for her accomplishment in having died. Something that I loved deeply about mom was that she was never afraid to try something new. Her death was about my grief, but it also was proof of her essential courage to keep going.

25

The gift of witnessing death

"The great business of life is to be, to do, to do without, and to depart."

— John Morley

About this gift

I had not experienced death as intimately as at this moment of mom's passing. It was, I think, mom's final gift to me, allowing me to witness something so essentially personal. She was preparing me for my own time of reckoning.

The night was dark, moonless and cold. Outside, beyond the window of mom's room, snow had stopped falling. Across the empty street, feeble strands of colored lights hung from the houses. It was Christmas night.

Mom lay in bed, her eyes closed. Her body was bathed in dim light filtering in from the hallway. She was either asleep or unconscious. The only sound was of her uneven breathing, heavy and raspy. This was the death rattle.

The world was quiet, devoid of all but the feeble life inside mom, and even that was about to fade into nothingness. I sat patiently at her side, next to my wife. We were entranced, even hypnotized, by the simplicity, the frailty and the repetition of the sound of her gasps.

Abruptly, mom stopped breathing. The silence shattered our dream-like isolation. My wife reached over and grasped my hand. Then just as suddenly, mom started to breathe again. But only for half a minute. Then she stopped forever.

Mom lay in her deathbed as still as a marble carving of herself. I went out to the hallway and called the nurse. She came in, looked at mom and said, simply, "She's gone."

There had been no high drama of last words or eternal promises. When death showed up, he entered the room on little cat's feet, like Carl Sandburg's fog.

Feelings shot through me: grief, relief, disbelief, terror, sadness and peace.

It had been 3,102 days since mom's advanced symptoms of Alzheimer's disease made her my responsibility. Back in 2007, by having agreed to be mom's guardian, I adopted as a child the woman who had raised me. The road we shared had been rocky, but filled with these unexpected gifts shared in this book. Now in this sober moment of her dying, I had thin comfort in knowing that I had seen it through to the end.

The nurse left the room so that we could spend time alone with the body. I placed my hand, almost in benediction, on her forehead, but pulled it away in shock. The skin was beginning to cool.

It was then that I had the immediate feeling of a more profound separation than I had ever experienced with her. Mom's eternal journey had begun. Now and forevermore, she would be silence and memory.

In the days that followed, I mourned other losses associated with my mother's death: chatter with the nurses, feeding my mother just as you feed an infant, wheeling her from floor to floor, where all the staff would shout, "Hi Shirley!" Mom loved being noticed and it gave me joy, too.

But at this exact moment of her death, one thing was crystal clear: We are defined as humans by our responsibilities to others. As a caretaker, what had begun as a burden now ended full of blessings.

26

The gift of granting final wishes

"Let the tent be struck."
— Robert E. Lee's last words before
dying

About this gift

*Death and burial are topics that make me
squirm. Many years before the onset of dementia,
Mom insisted on discussing her final "disposal"
with me in very concrete terms. Her straightforward ideas and her frequent discussions slowly
eroded my avoidance of the topic, based on my
own terror of death and dying, and replaced my
fears with practicality and humor. Through all
of this conversation, her final wishes eventually
became clear to her and to me, and that clarity
was a gift not only in lessening my own fears of
death, but also in removing any uncertainty of
what she wanted me to do after she died.*

Most people (such as myself) are afraid of dying
and avoid any concrete reminder of mortality,
such as a discussion regarding the disposition of their
final remains. Mom, on the contrary, seemed almost

obsessed with settling the issue of her final resting place. Because I was her executor, it was a frequent topic of conversation between us, starting at a relatively young age and continuing until she began to show signs of Alzheimer's.

All along, mom kept re-evaluating her decision and changing it.

One thing remained constant: she wished to be cremated. "I don't want to be cold and I don't want worms crawling inside me," she said emphatically. The alternative, burial of her prepared body, preceded by reviewal, meant that she would have to assign her makeup to a third party, not at all to her liking, and subject herself to indefensible critique. "I can just imagine all my friends filing by the coffin and then huddling in the cloakroom, making nasty comments about my wrinkles, hair coloring or lipstick. I couldn't bear it." Cremation was a settle thing.

"They wouldn't do such a thing!" I said.

"Yes they would, and I would do the same thing. I don't want them to get the last word."

"But you'll be dead, mom" I said.

"Doesn't matter. I'll know, and their petty comments will be bouncing inside my head for eternity."

Thus all scenarios of her final disposition began with cremation as a fixed and non-negotiable starting point. Deciding where to deposit her ashes was more difficult and more changeable.

For a long time she wanted her ashes spread on an idyllic city lake in Minneapolis, where mom had spent time with family and friends.

Then, years later, while we were enjoying a salmon dinner, she asked, "Do you think the fish will eat my ashes?"

"Which fish?"

"The ones in Lake Harriet, where my ashes will be spread."

"No," I said.

"Doesn't matter, seems too gruesome of a possibility. How about the Southdale Mall?" I must have looked at her with some surprise, because she began to justify her new idea. "I love to shop. Maybe place me in a planter near the center of the mall, where there is commotion. I want to be among people and activity. I don't want to be alone."

"Mom, I'm pretty sure that would be illegal."

"Who has to know?"

So there it stood, until she remarried, and she and Edgar moved to Phoenix. She changed her mind again. "I decided on a place to be buried. A niche," she said to me by phone.

"What in the world is a niche?" I asked her.

"Oh, it's a beautiful solution. I just bought a niche down here, in a wall facing the sun. It's like a tiny storage compartment. A cubby. You put my ashes in the cubby and my name goes on the door. I'll be above ground. No fish. No worms. And I'll be warm."

"Isn't this like stuffing you in a locker at the gym?" I asked. "You hate exercise."

"No, it's much more sophisticated. It's French. A niche." She pronounced it "neeesch," with great satisfaction.

So it was resolved for another decade, until mom called me from Phoenix and announced she wasn't going to be eternalized in the French wall after all.

"Why?"

"I'll be too lonely. I think Ed really wants his ashes to be spread on the family lake in Latvia, so where does that leave me? I don't want to be down here all by myself, with no one to visit me and talk to me, with all of you children in Minnesota or California, and California is out of the question. I hate earthquakes."

She had now decided that she wanted her urn to be buried in a plot next to her parents, who were interred in a small but quaint and remote Jewish cemetery in Duluth.

"Now you're back to being in the ground. What about the worms?" I asked.

"I'll be in a brass urn. I've picked it out. I'll be safe."

"What about the sunshine and not wanting to

be cold. More than half the year that cemetery in Duluth is under two feet of snow."

"But I'll be with grandma and grandpa."

"Hardly a soul visits the place. I thought you wanted crowds."

"I did, but as you get older, more and more you want to be left alone. You want peace and quiet."

Had not Alzheimer's soon gummed up her thinking process, mom might have changed her mind again, but this was the last she spoke of it. Fortunately, I typed her words and had her affix her signature, so I could follow through without question. Mom's certainty, or what would now have to suffice for certainty, was an immense gift to me in that I did not have to guess after she was gone.

The real gift to me was her morbid sense of humor. Although she was always serious, I thought this on-going discussion, in a way, poked fun at death, or at least took it in practical strides. The more we talked, the less mysterious death became. Instead of something unknowing, terrifying and secret, death became practical and out in the open. It lessened my own fears of being mortal in the context of eternity.

And, so it is. Mom got her wish. She resides within a few feet of the once beating hearts of her mother and father. They huddle together beneath tall pine and spruce, among a handful of other friends from the small and disappearing Jewish community in Duluth. I love visiting her grave, especially in the winter, where my deep footprints in the snow are the only signs of remembrance.

Otherwise, silence and peace are constant companions of her sacred dust, for all of time.

27

The gift of a lasting image

"God gave us memories that we might have roses in December."

James M. Barrie

About this gift

I make a habit of remembering the last time — or a last memorable time — that I have seen somebody. These memories of last remembrances of people are gifts to me, because over time they become fixed and reliable and cherished: They are the gift of permanence in an impermanent world.

I have a collection of last images. These are memories I have of the way I last saw someone. Or nearly last saw them. I think this is about not wanting to let anyone go.

The last memory I have of my father, for example, is of him standing at the picture window of his home, looking out at my car as I backed out and drove away. Before I could come visit him again, he died of a heart attack.

What I remember most about my father in that image were his eyes. His look was sad and lonely. His health had deteriorated. He hung on by a thread of stubborn determination. As he stood in the window, I knew he was sad that I was leaving him, and he was sad that he was about to be leaving life, because he knew his poor body could not continue to survive much longer.

Straining my neck as I started the car up the street, I watched my father grow distant. I wanted to take him with me. I have taken him with me. He is with me now, but it is not quite the same. Anyway, that is my last memory of my father.

I have one of mom, too. When I came to visit her, I would get off the elevator and, while still out in the hallway, I could see her at a distance by looking through the open doorway of the common room. She sat in her wheelchair, dressed always smartly, her arms folded together on her lap, looking forward, listening to the sounds around her, for she could not see.

She was trying to engage, small and confusing as her world had become. By the furl of her brow, I knew she listened intently for some clue that would give her a connection to life. Her hair was ruffled from having been quickly brushed. Her eyes, once deeply brown, were milky. But her profile was composed, still and beautiful. Her beauty never left her as she aged.

I remember mom in this patient pose. She was, indeed, a profile in quiet courage. She didn't know where she was. She couldn't see. Her mind was a jumble. She had no sense of time or place. Yet she sat there, listening, trying to engage. She sat like this for hours at a time.

After watching her from afar, I went to her, passing through the hallway and entering the common room. I came up to her and said as softly as possible, so as not to startle her, "Hi Mom, it's me. Rick." And she said with great surprise and enthusiasm, "Rick! Where have you been? It's been so long since I've seen you." She grabbed my hand and squeezed it hard. "I'm so glad you're here," she said.

And then the words left her. She could not think of anything more to say. But it didn't matter. I heard all I needed to hear. That will be my last memory of mom, and it will sustain me forever.

CPSIA information can be obtained
at www.ICGtesting.com
Printed in the USA
FFOW03n0456081117
43386242-41980FF